SUGAR SKULLS

COLORING BOOK

ARTWORK BY JENNIFER KAU

This Book belongs to:

____

SUGAR SKULLS, VOLUME 1
JENNTANLGED COLORING BOOKS

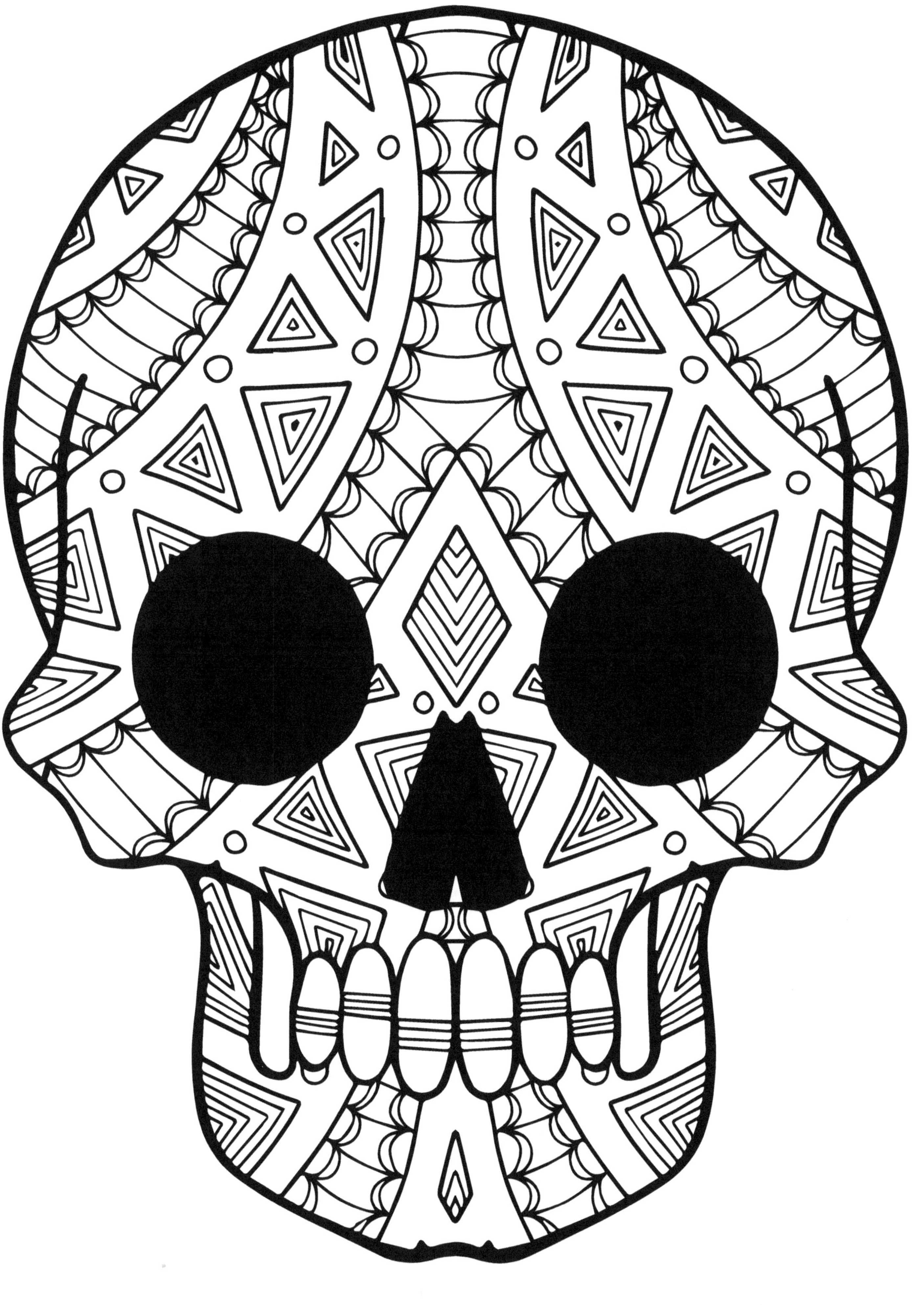

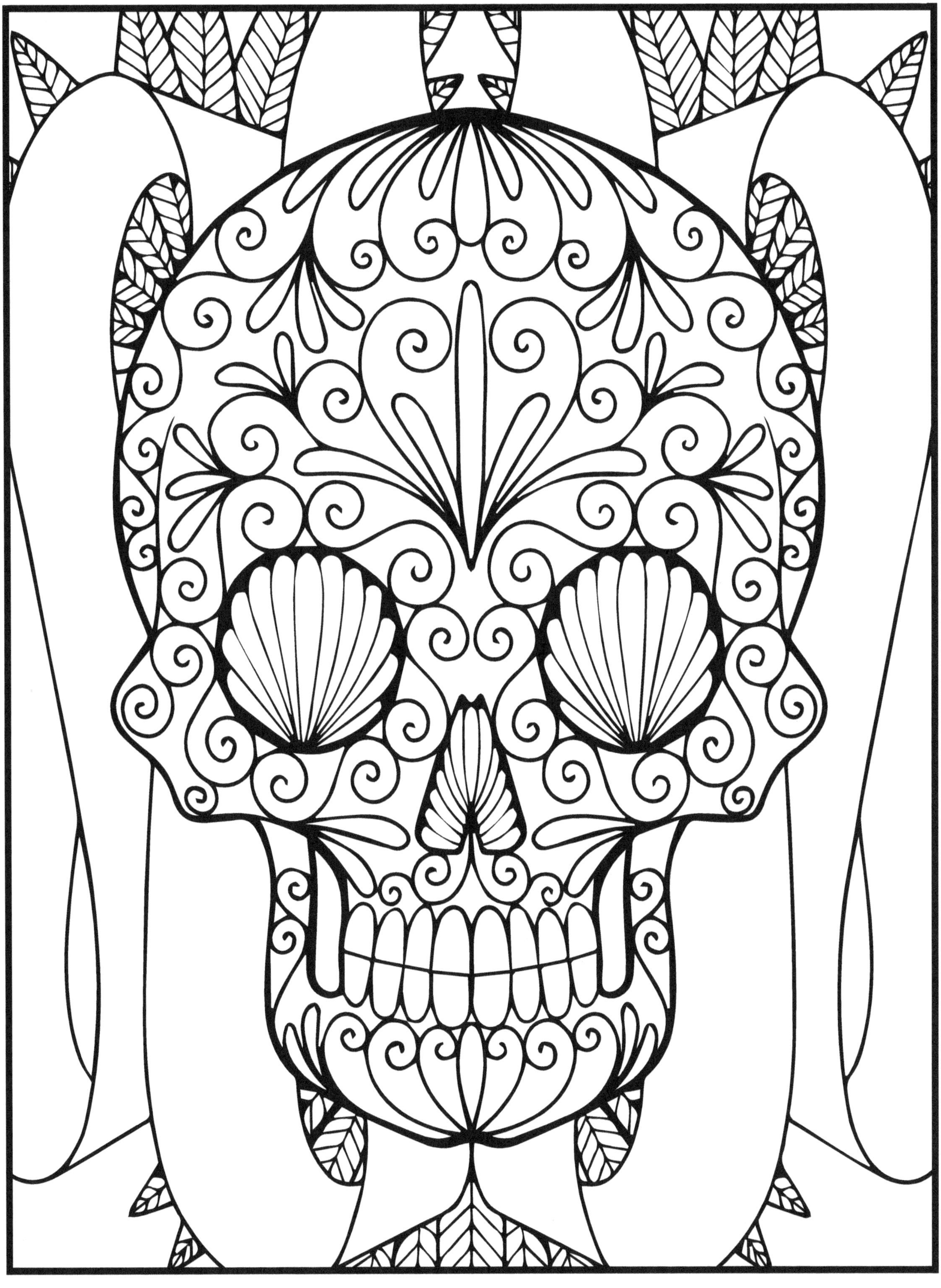

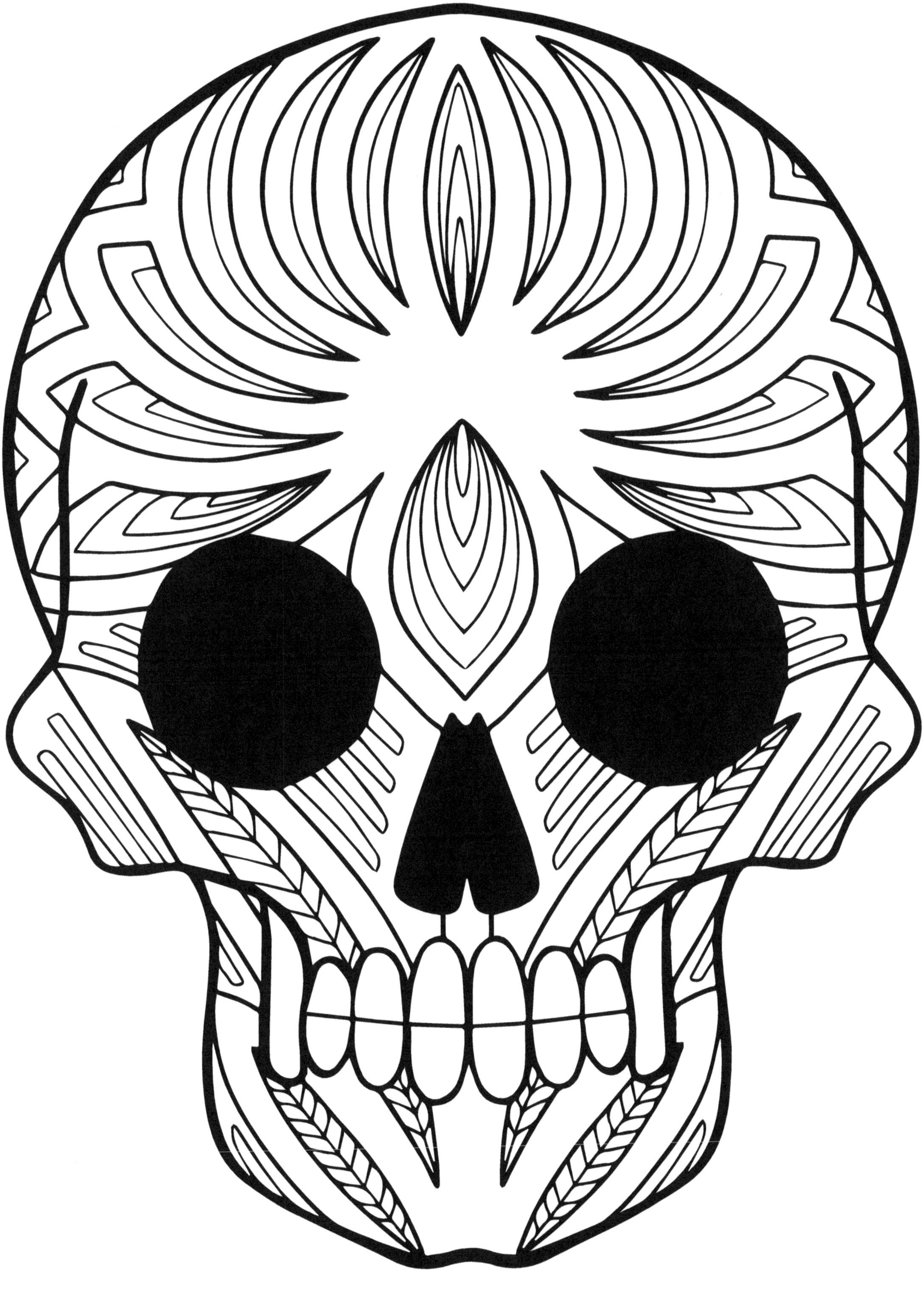

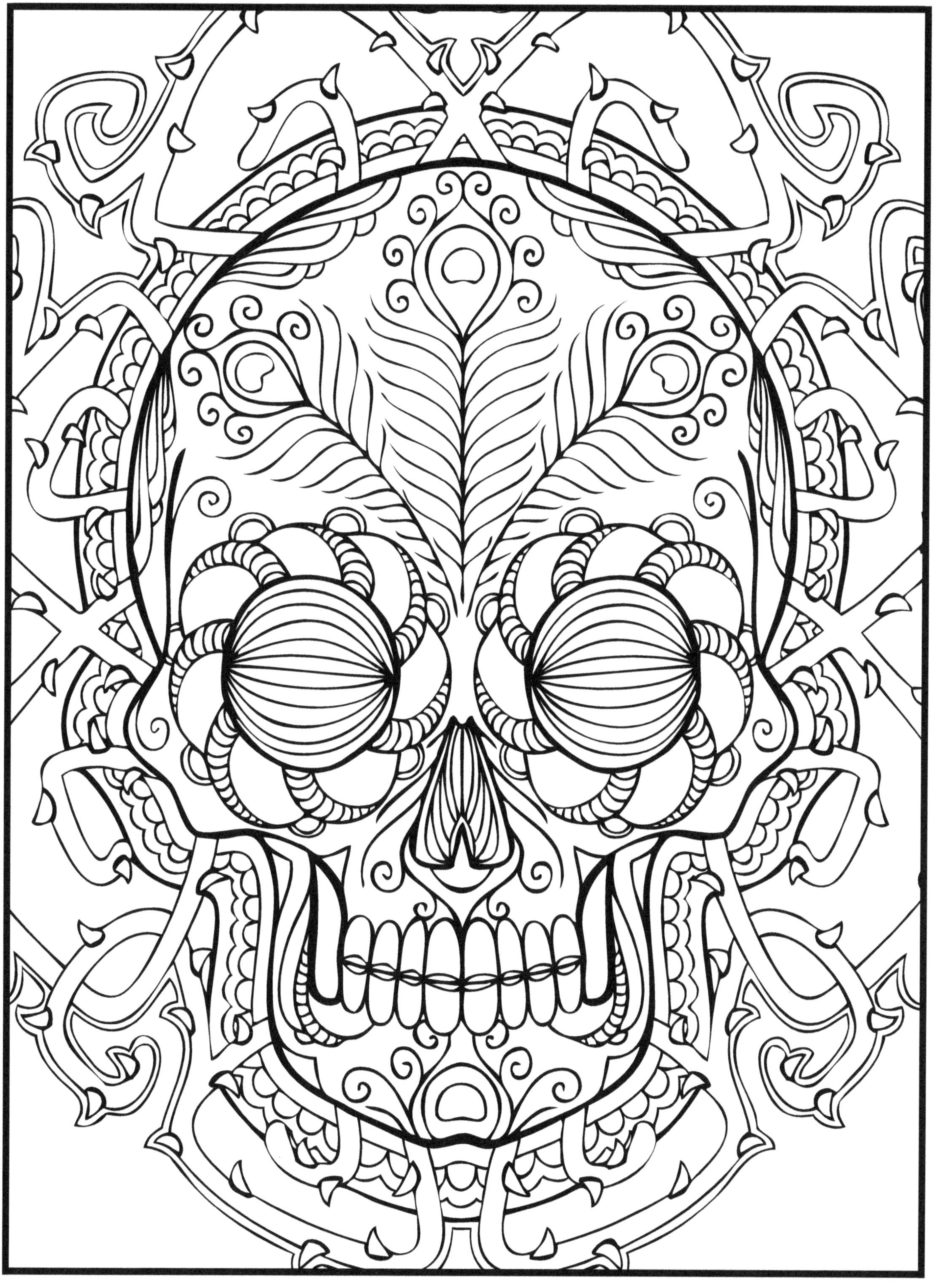

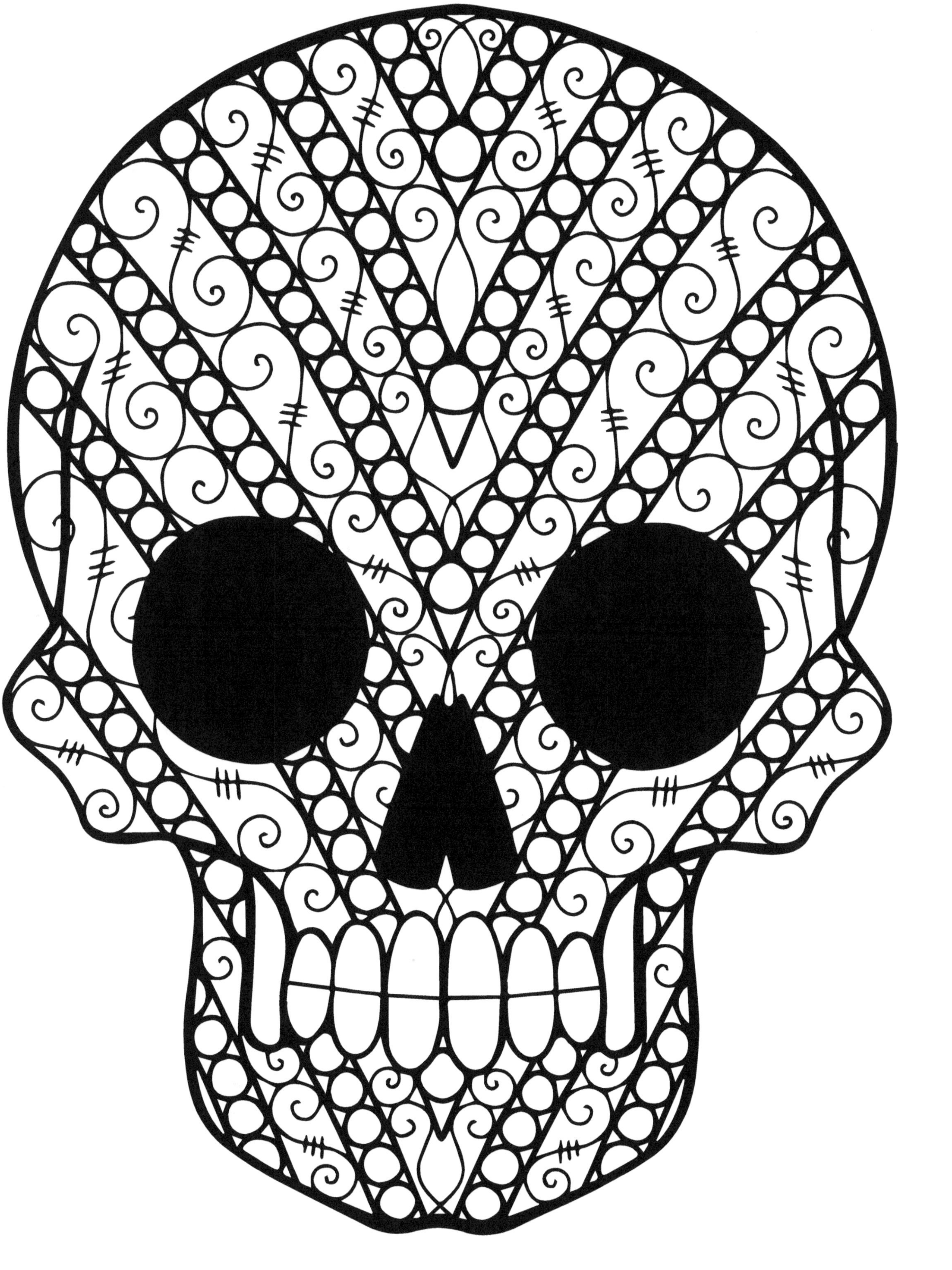

www.ingramcontent.com/pod-product-compliance
Lightning Source LLC
Chambersburg PA
CBHW081516040426
42447CB00013B/3245
9780692860007